AF227464

This book is dedicated to everyone impacted by cerebral palsy.
Thank you to everyone who helped to inform the book by sharing their own experiences.

Second Edition
First Published 2023
Tiny Tree Children's Books
West Wing Studios, Unit 166
The Mall, Luton, LU1 2TL

tinytreebooks.com

Illustrations © 2023 Adam Walker-Parker

My Child Has Cerebral Palsy

Written by
Alex Winstanley

Illustrated by
Adam Walker-Parker

My child has cerebral palsy,
but what do those words mean?
Let's talk it through together.
Come along; I'll set the scene.

I have a group of friends
and there's something that we share.

Our children have cerebral palsy,
so our stories we compare.

age 6

age 14

age 22

age 34

CP is a lifelong condition.
It affects the muscles and brain.
This changes the way someone moves
and puts the body under strain.

Sometimes when babies are born
their brains may not get enough air,
or they could be born too early,
so they might need some extra care.

Growing up, my child felt 'different'
to the children he saw each day.
Though as he grew up he noticed
that we are all 'different' in some way.

My child uses a wheelchair
which helps him to get around.
He loves giving rides to family
and racing friends on the playground.

STORE

CP has meant that my child
lives her life at her own pace.
For us this is our 'normal',
as are the obstacles we face.

One of my children uses splints
and equipment as he walks.
His brother uses an app
that helps him when he talks.

HELLO!

Daily exercises
help to relax my child's hand.
He's had lots of operations
so that he is able to stand.

My child likes to be asked questions.
He loves to speak with friends.

Some still talk to him through me,
though they know how to make amends.

HAPPY SMILES TRAINING
DISABILITY AWARENESS

My child wants people to listen
to her thoughts and how she feels.
She wants the same life chances,
even if she moves using wheels.

My child who has CP
faces other challenges too.
But we all face our own struggles,
which *together* we can come through.

My child has cerebral palsy.
Now you know about it too.

When you meet someone with cerebral palsy
you'll know just what to do.

About the Author

My name is Alex Winstanley. I am an author, teacher and social entrepeneur from Wigan, England. My background as a teacher, as well as a carer to young disabled adults, has shaped my outlook on the inclusion of disabled people and those with long-term health conditions across society. Through my books I aim to raise awareness of a range of long-term health conditions in a positive and supportive way for children and young people. I am extremely passionate about promoting a diverse and inclusive society in which every person is valued and celebrated. Each one of my books is inspired by real people as I believe there is nothing more important than giving a voice to those with lived experience.

@alexwinstanleyauthor

/alexwinstanleyauthor

@alexwauthor

About the Illustrator

My name is Adam Walker-Parker. I am an artist and illustrator represented by Lemonade Illustration Agency from the Cairngorm National Park in the Highlands of Scotand. I focus on creating illustrations for books that are fun and engaging and that hel p to raise awareness of many health conditions. I enjoy creating images with inclusion and diversity in mind.

www.awalkerparker.com

My Grandma Has Dementia

Written by
Alex Winstanley

Illustrated by
Adam Walker-Parker

2021 Dementia Hero Awards Winner!